Simple and Fun™

SCIENCE

BOOK A

Grade K - 1

Authors

Lynn Wicker

Dennis McKee

Cover Design,

Text Layout, & Graphics

Ed Francis

Consultants

Michael B. Leyden

Todd Fenemore

Introduction to Simple and Fun Science

Science is a word that comes from a Latin term that means "to know." In order to really know, children need to experience, to investigate, to touch, to hold, and to question. An ancient Chinese philosopher once said:

"What I hear, I forget. What I see, I remember. What I do, I know."

When children can hear, see, and do, they can begin to understand. This book was written to encourage children to investigate, to explore, and to question.

Education in science is a multi-faceted adventure. Children need to learn how to "do science." This occurs as they develop Process Skills. Process Skills are methods of inquiry that help them in all academic areas of the curriculum. Some people call them "life skills" because they are used in many daily activities from baking a cake to mowing the lawn. During the process of gathering, interpreting data, and applying information about their physical and biological and earth science environment, children master the science process skills.

These are the Process Skills we have made every attempt to nurture in this series:

Recalling
Measuring
Graphing
Communicating
Observing
Inferring
Analyzing
Classifying
Predicting
Summarizing
Setting Goals
Gathering Data
Interpreting Data

As children learn and improve their Process Skills, they are simultaneously learning the physical, biological, and earth-science content and the subject, and they are involved in critical and creative problem solving. Using the Process Skills the children are enhancing and improving their critical thinking and creative thinking. They are:

- **using past observations to predict future events;**
- **performing simple experiments in an effort to find answers to questions, and new questions;**
- **verifying an explanation to check it out;**
- **applying knowledge and reasoning in decision making and problem solving;**
- **using science method and experience to explain observations and solve problems; and**
- **developing new questions and searching for solutions to problems.**

This book is filled with fun and fascinating things to do in science. Some of the activities in the book will help children understand an idea. Some activities will help children think of new questions. As you and your child (children) are working through the book, here are some general rules for being a "good" scientist, and for that matter, a good learner.

Make sure children:

1. Pay attention to the work from start to finish.
2. Clean equipment before and after an activity.
   Keep things clean and put things away when finished.
3. Label containers in experiments.
4. Work with a partner or an adult helper. Scientists usually work in teams.

5. Think about safety first. Here are some tips:
   Never look directly at the sun.
   Protect your eyes from anything that can splatter or shatter.
   Never get close to animals in the wild or even strange pets.
   Never taste anything unless you know exactly what it is and that it is safe.
   Stay away from fire, burners, very hot water, or anything that can burn.
   Be very careful with scissors and ask an adult helper when using any cutting tool.
6. Keep a science response journal. Write down questions when they arise. Write down observations. Interpret and represent explanations of concepts and new information in their own words. Draw pictures of observations. Design experiments and new investigations.
7. Take time. Try not to hurry. Try not to get frustrated. If something doesn't work the first time, try again. Everyone makes mistakes. Sometimes failures in science raise new questions and uncover new solutions. And, sometimes solutions to problems cause new problems requiring new solutions.
8. Stay organized.

Before you and/or children start any activity or experiment:

Read through the activity first.
Gather all the materials that will be needed for any activity.
Follow each step. Don't skip steps.

As children do an activity or experiment guide them to:

Be very accurate.
Be very careful and work cautiously.
Be very neat so the work and the work area are neat and clean.
Be creative.

The Essential Learning Products Science Series encourages children to work at their own pace. Book A is intended for children from ages 4 through 6. Use it as a supplement to existing curricula in the classroom or independently at home. Try not to impose your own conclusions on the children. Stand back and allow the child to find out. However, they do need your guidance.

The authors and publisher have made every reasonable effort that the activities within this book are safe when conducted as instructed. When appropriate, the authors have suggested a step be conducted by an adult and not a child. The authors and publisher assume no responsibility for any damage caused or sustained while performing the activities in this book. Supervise young readers working with the activities in this book.

Table of Contents

Observing

Carefully look at these pages for one minute. Then turn the page to answer some questions about what you observed.

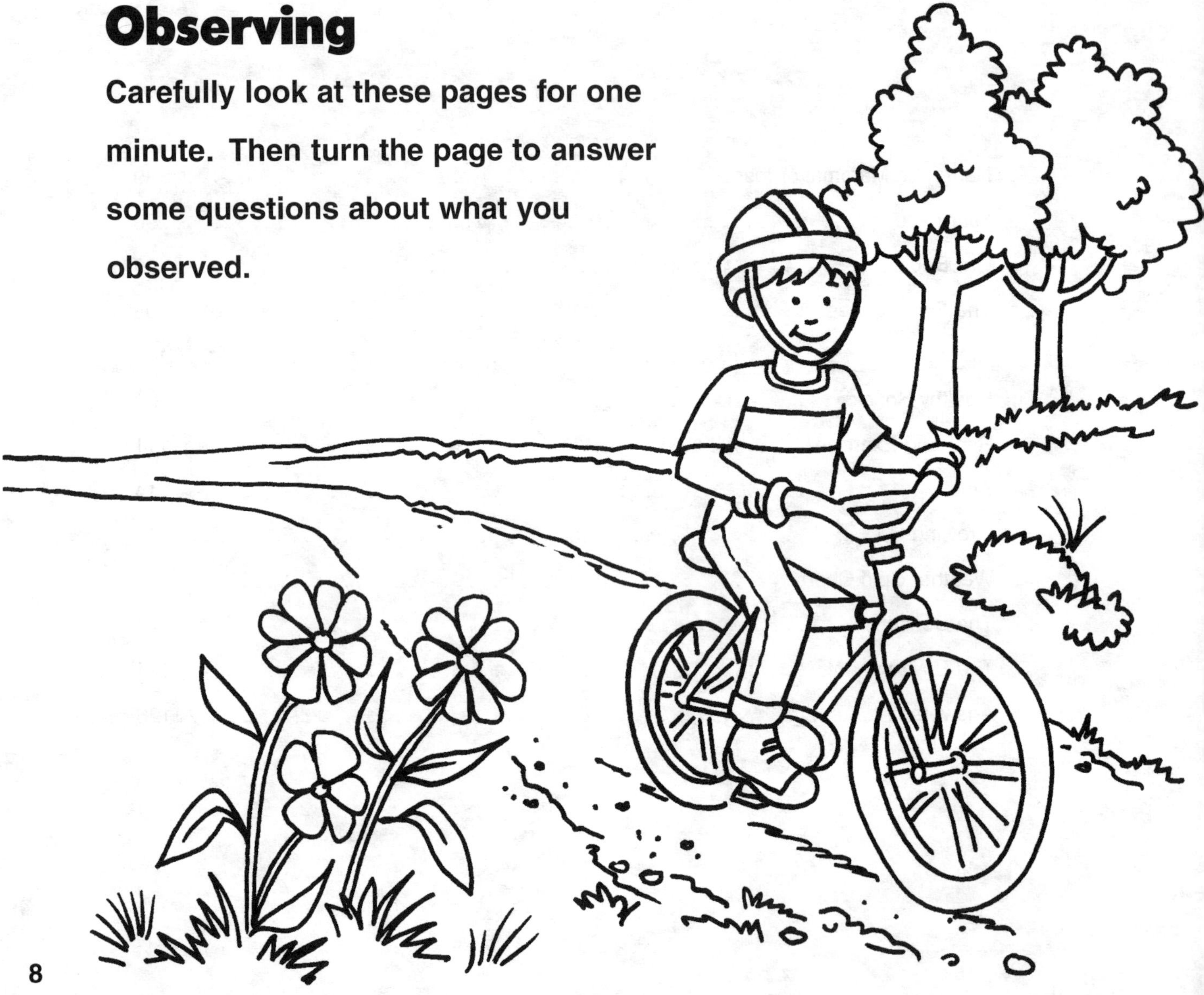

Park Observation Questions

Without looking back at the picture, place an X by the correct match.

Who was riding the bike?	________**boy**	________**girl**
Who was flying the kite?	________**boy**	________**girl**
Who was eating the nut?	________**elephant**	________**squirrel**
Who was in the pond?	________**duck**	________**frog**

Park Observation Questions

Fill in the correct number for each object without looking back at the picture.

1. How many trees were in the picture? ________

2. How many flowers were in the picture? ________

3. How many birds were in the picture? ________

4. How many ducks were in the picture? ________

5. How many frogs were in the picture? ________

Observing

Carefully study the picture for one minute. Then turn the page to see how well you remember what you observed.

Beach Observation Questions

Answer the following questions without looking back at the picture.

1. **How many pails were in the picture?** __________
2. **How many shovels were in the picture?** __________
3. **How many children were in the picture?** __________
4. **How many sand castles were in the picture?** __________

Sorting

Many things can be sorted into groups in several different ways.

This activity will demonstrate how sorting works.

What you need:

- following pages
- scissors
- coloring pencils or crayons

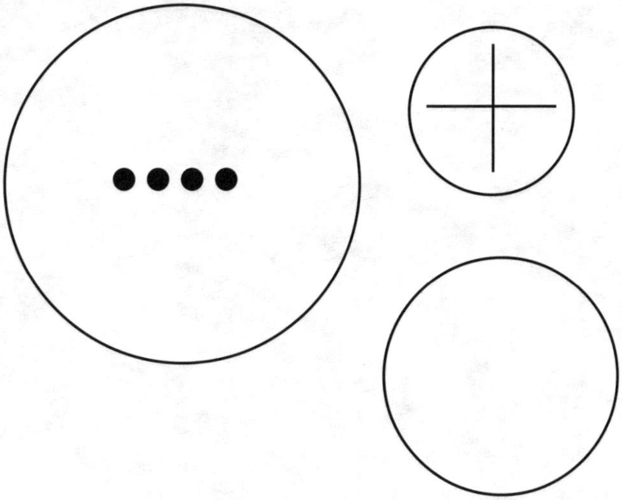

What to do:

1. Carefully color and cut out the shapes on the following page.
2. Sort the shapes by shape.
3. Sort the shapes by size.
4. Sort the shapes by design.
5. Sort the shapes by color.

Sorting

Things can be sorted any way we see they are alike.

Sort these balls by drawing a line connecting each different group.

Object Sorting

What you need:

a pencil	a weed	a crayon
a plant	a toy	a book
a shoe	a spoon	grass

What to do:

1. Gather all the materials listed above.
2. Sort the objects into two groups.

   Group 1 will be objects that are alive.

   Group 2 will be objects that are not alive.
3. List the objects under the correct heading on the next page.

LIVING	NON-LIVING

Sorting

Nature Walk

Take a nature walk around your neighborhood. Look for things that are alive and not alive. Collect the things you find that are not alive in a bag. After the walk, sort the things that are not alive into two groups. Group A will be things that were alive at one time. For example, a stick was alive when it was part of a tree. Group B will be things that never were alive.

For example, a piece of metal was never alive.

Comparing

Finding the Differences

The pictures on the next two pages are similar, but there are at least five things that are different in the second picture. Circle the five differences. Hint: Look for things that have been added to the picture. Look for things that have been taken away from the picture.

Comparing

Leaf Rub

What you need:

- several leaves (from different kinds of trees)
- crayons
- paper

What to do:

1. Collect several green leaves from different kinds of trees.
2. Place a leaf under the next page in this book.
3. Rub a crayon on top of the paper that is over the leaf until you can see the outline of the whole leaf.
4. Repeat steps 2 and 3 using extra sheets of paper for your other leaves.
5. Compare the leaf rub pictures by seeing how the leaves are alike.
6. Compare the leaf rub pictures by seeing how the leaves are different.

First Leaf Rub

Comparing

Leaf Rub

Ways the leaves are alike:

Ways the leaves are different:

Recording

Coin Flip

We can practice recording what we observe with a simple activity.

What you need:

coin pencil

What to do:

1. Flip a coin in the air.
2. Observe how it lands -- heads or tails.
3. Record your observation on the chart on the next page.
4. Repeat steps 1 through 3 until the chart is complete.

Coin Flip Chart

Coin Flip	Heads or Tails	
First flip	Heads	Tails
Second flip	Heads	Tails
Third flip	Heads	Tails
Fourth flip	Heads	Tails
Fifth flip	Heads	Tails
Sixth flip	Heads	Tails
Seventh flip	Heads	Tails
Eighth flip	Heads	Tails
Ninth flip	Heads	Tails
Tenth flip	Heads	Tails

Total number of Heads circled ______________

Total number of Tails circled ______________

Animals

The following are different types of animals.

Birds:

Birds have feathers and wings. Birds lay eggs. Most birds can fly.

Fish:

Fish have scales on their bodies. Fish must swim underwater all the time. Most fish lay eggs.

Mammals:

Mammals have hair or fur on their bodies. Mammals nurse their babies. Mammals are warm-blooded.

Reptiles:

Reptiles can live on land or in the water. Most reptiles hatch from eggs. Most reptiles have skin with scales.

Amphibians:

Amphibians must have water to lay their eggs. Most amphibian babies grow in the water.

Match the animals with their babies.

Match each animal with the sound it makes.

meow

moo

oink

ruff-ruff

Classifying

Classify the Animals

Color all the animals. Cut out the following pictures. Group the pictures into groups of birds, fish, mammals, amphibians, and reptiles. Paste them onto the following pages by the group in which they belong. Explain why you grouped them together.

Birds

Fish

Mammals

Reptiles

Amphibians

Animals

How Animals Move

Some animals move by running. Some animals hop. Some animals fly in the air. Some animals swim in the water. And some animals slither on the ground.

See if you can run outside like the animals that run. Show how the hopping animals hop. Can you swim? If not, can you learn to swim? Try to slither on the ground. Which way was the easiest for you to move? Why?

Animals are different and they move in the way that is easiest for them.

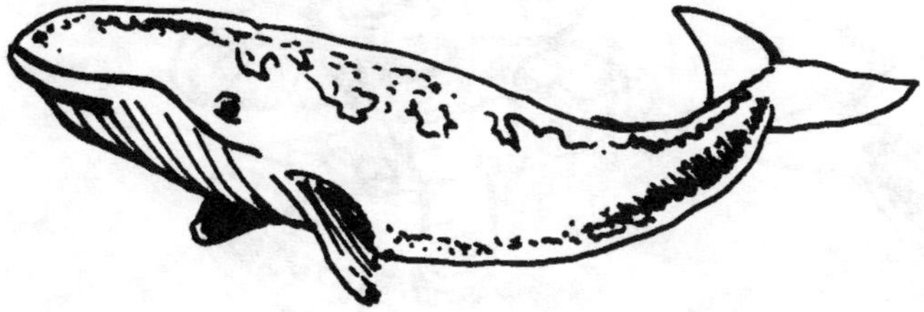

Circle the animals that move best by hopping.

Color all the animals.

Draw an X by the animals that move best by running.

Color all the animals.

Circle the animals that move best by flying.

Color all the animals.

Draw an X by the picture of the animal that moves best by slithering. Color all the animals.

Draw an X by the pictures of the animals that move best by swimming. Color all the animals

Plants

What are plants? Plants grow almost every place on earth. Plants are things such as grass, shrubs, flowers, and trees. All plants have roots. The roots take in water from the soil. The water is carried up the stem or trunk to the leaves. Have you ever seen a plant that has wilted and looks like it is falling over?

Identifying Plants

Place an X by each flower in the picture below. Circle each tree in the picture below. Color the pictures of the plants.

The Importance of Plants

We could not live on Earth without plants. Plants make the oxygen in the air we breathe. Even the food we eat is either a plant, comes from a plant, or comes from an animal that eats plants.

Plant Questions

Circle the correct answer to the following questions.

1. Plants provide us with oxygen.	yes	no
2. We can eat plants.	yes	no
3. We do not need plants to live.	yes	no
4. Grass is a kind of plant.	yes	no

Parts of a Plant

Draw a line connecting the part of the plant to its part on the picture.

flower

stem

root

leaf

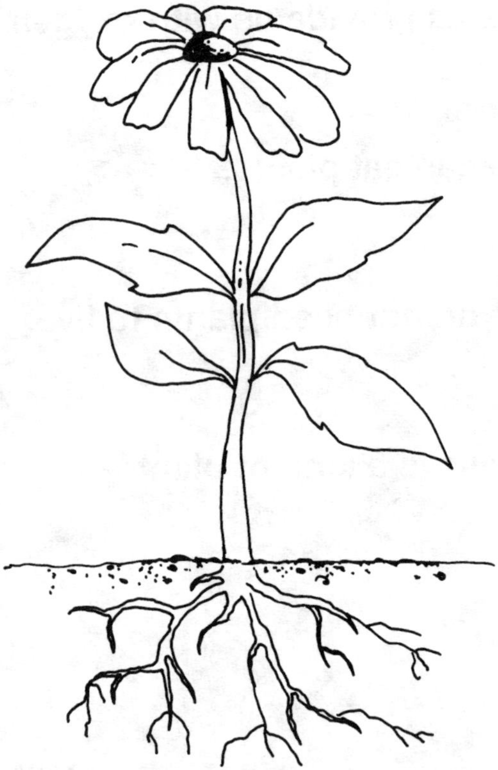

Parts of a Tree

Draw a line connecting the part of the tree to its part on the picture.

trunk

roots

leaves

Growing a Bean

What you need:

- bean seeds (Lima beans work great, but any dry bean should work)
- paper towel
- plastic bag with a zip closure
- water
- ruler
- windowsill

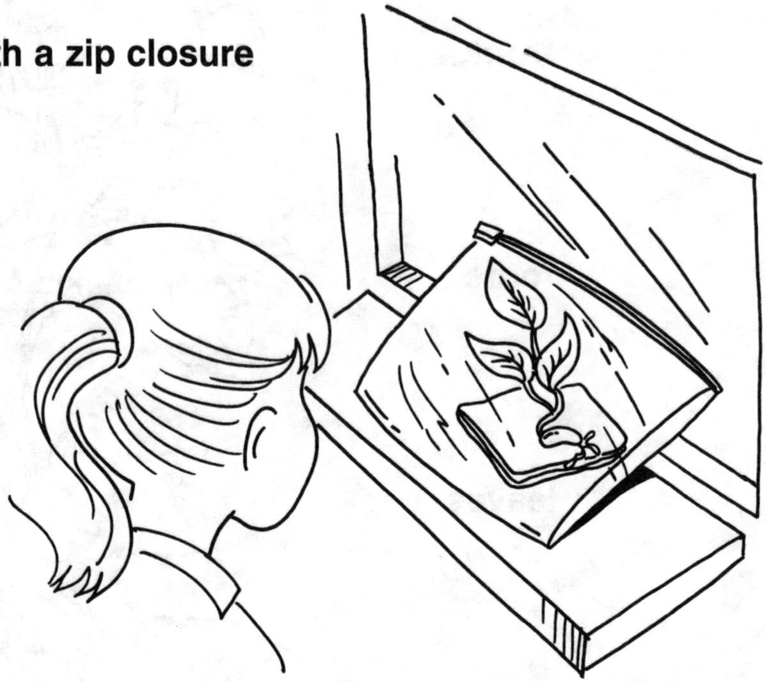

What to do:

1. Fold the paper towel in half.
2. Fold it in half again.
3. Fold it in half two more times.

4. Get the folded paper towel very wet with water, but not dripping.
5. Place the wet, folded paper towel in the plastic bag.

6. Place the bean on the wet paper towel in the bag.
7. Seal the bag closed.
8. Leave the bag on a windowsill for several days.
9. Observe the growth of the bean each day.
10. Measure the length of the bean with a ruler.

Bean Growth Questions

1. What did you notice the first day?

____

2. Can you see where the roots are?

____

3. Did the leaves appear?

____

4. How long did it take for the leaves to appear?

____

5. What happened to the bean?

____

6. Measure the bean root each day.

Day 1_____ Day 2_____ Day 3_____

Day 4_____ Day 5_____ Day 6_____

Plants Need Water

A wilted plant is usually a plant that does not have enough water. Water is what holds up a plant. As long as there is enough water to flow through the stem, the stem will stand up straight. If there is not enough water, the stem cannot hold itself up.

How do plants get water to their leaves?

What you need:

a glass of water (about 1 to 2 inches of water only)

a celery stalk

food coloring (Blue or red works best.)

a spoon

a knife (Have an adult use this.)

What to do:

1. Put the food coloring in the glass of water until it turns the water a dark color.
2. Stir the water.
3. Remove the spoon from the glass and place it in a sink.
4. Have an adult cut off the bottom of the celery stalk about one inch.
5. Place the celery stalk in the glass with the cut end down.
6. Watch the food coloring as it goes up the celery stalk.

Celery Leaf Experiment Questions

1. What happened to the food coloring? (Have you seen a plant that has wilted and looks like it is falling over?)

2. Why do you think this happened?

3. Do you think all plants get water from the soil this way?

4. Where do you think the water enters the plant first, the stem or the roots?

Growing Grass

Humpty Dumpty Grass Garden

What you need:

- empty pint milk carton
- half of an empty eggshell
- black marker or crayon
- tape
- markers
- water
- topsoil or dirt
- red construction paper
- grass seeds
- scissors
- tablespoon

What to do:

1. Rinse out the milk carton.
2. Cut the top spout parts off of the carton.
3. Cut the red construction paper to fit around the outside of the carton.
4. Tape the construction paper in place with a small piece of tape. (You should now have a red box without a top.)
5. Use the black marker or crayon to draw bricks on the red construction paper.
6. Fill the carton with dirt and topsoil.
7. Carefully fill the eggshell with dirt.
8. Put a face on the eggshell with the markers.

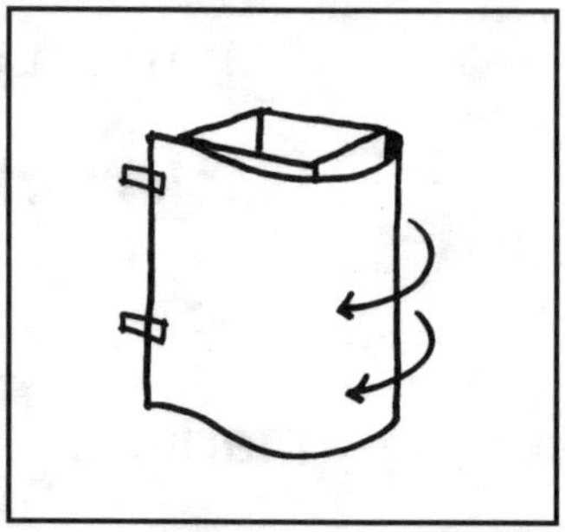

9. Set the eggshell with dirt carefully in a corner of the carton dirt side up.

10. Carefully spread grass seed in the eggshell only. Do not let any fall into the carton.
11. Cover the grass seed with a thin layer of dirt.

12. Add about 3 tablespoons of water to the grass seed.
13. Place it in a sunny spot and add a little water every other day.
14. Use scissors to give Humpty Dumpty a haircut when he needs it.

Humpty Dumpty Grass Garden Questions

1. How many grass seeds did you plant?

2. How many days did it take until you saw the sprouts?

3. What color was the grass?

4. Does the grass stop growing when you cut it?

5. Does the eggshell grow also?

6. Is the grass living or non-living?

7. Is the soil living or non-living?

8. What do you think would happen if you didn't water the grass?

9. What do you think would happen if you cut the grass too short?

Classification

Color all of the plants colors of green. Color the flowers bright colors. Colo

all of the animals the colors you think they really are.

Classifying Objects

Circle the things you think are alive. Color all of the objects.

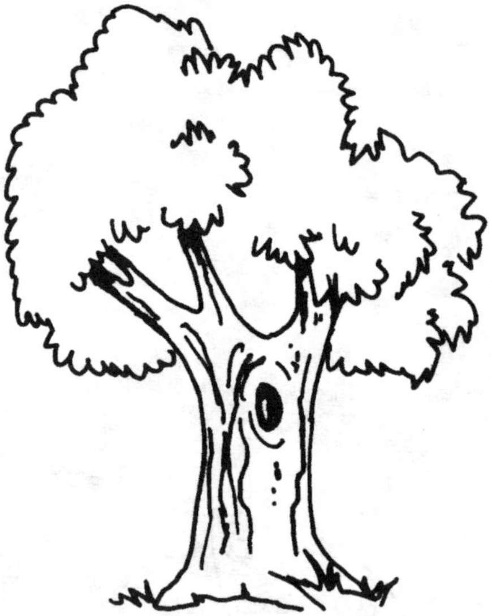

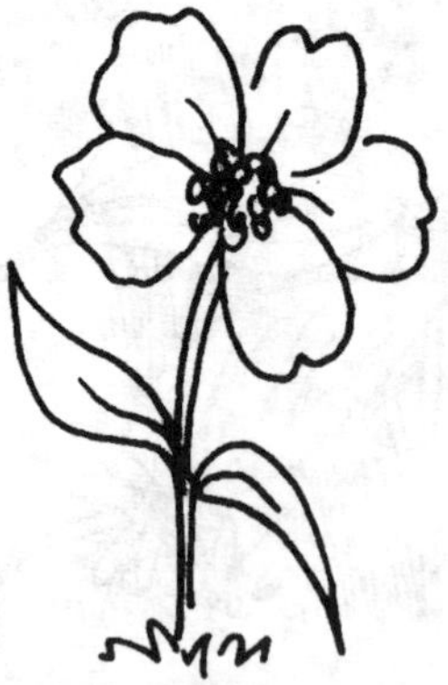

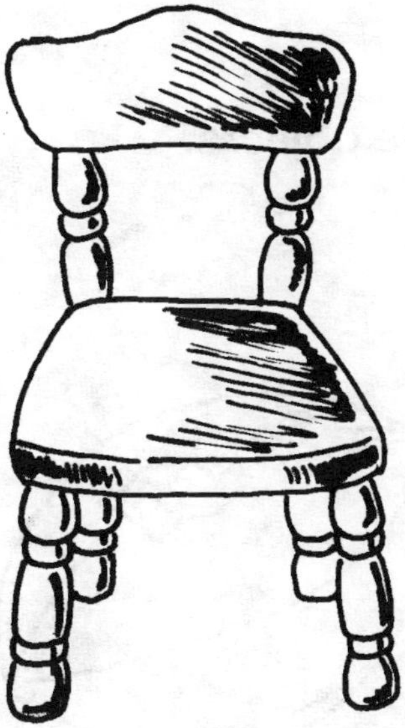

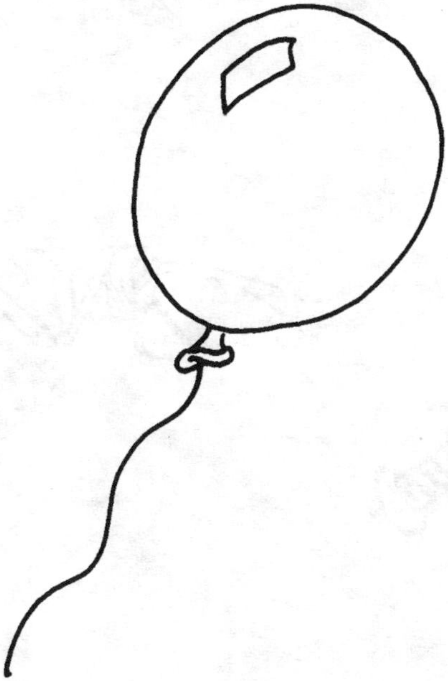

Classifying Objects

Put an X by each object that is not alive. Color all of the objects.

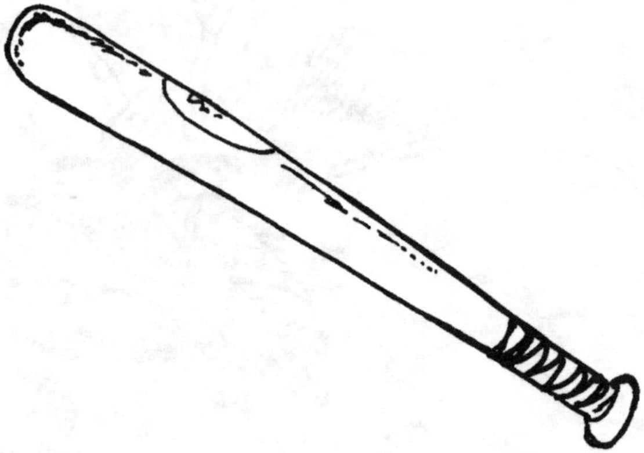

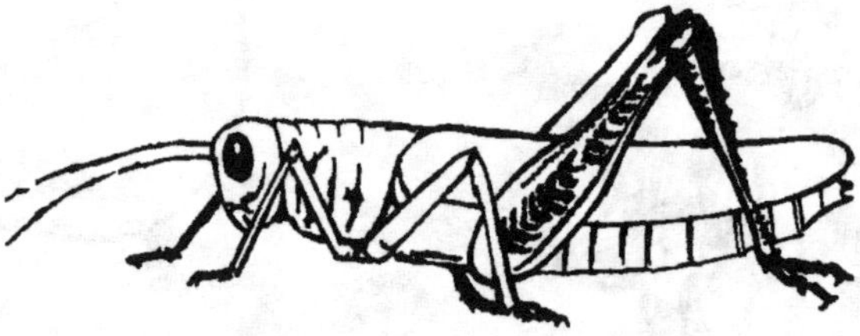

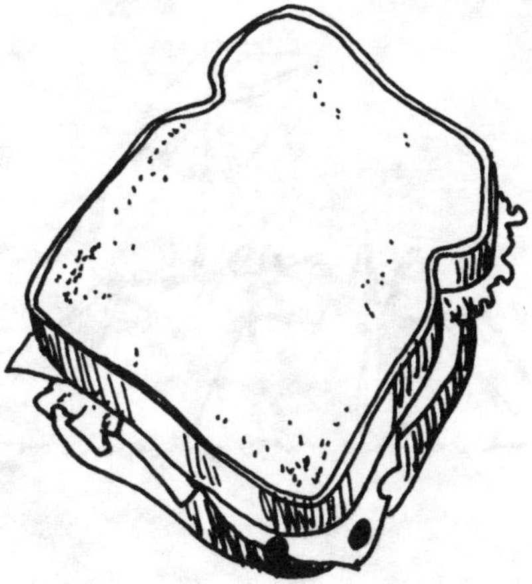

Ants

Ants are very hard workers. Most ants are called worker ants. There is one queen ant for each ant colony. An ant colony is the name for a large group of ants that all live and work together. The queen ant stays inside the colony while the worker ants dig tunnels and hunt for food to bring back to the queen ant.

An ant can carry many times its own weight in food. If you were an ant, you could lift an adult.

Sometimes two or three ants will work together to carry one large piece of food back to the queen ant.

All ants have three body sections and six legs. Some types of ants also have wings, but usually just the queen ant has wings.

Draw a line to the correct parts of the ant.

head **body** **abdomen**

(thorax)

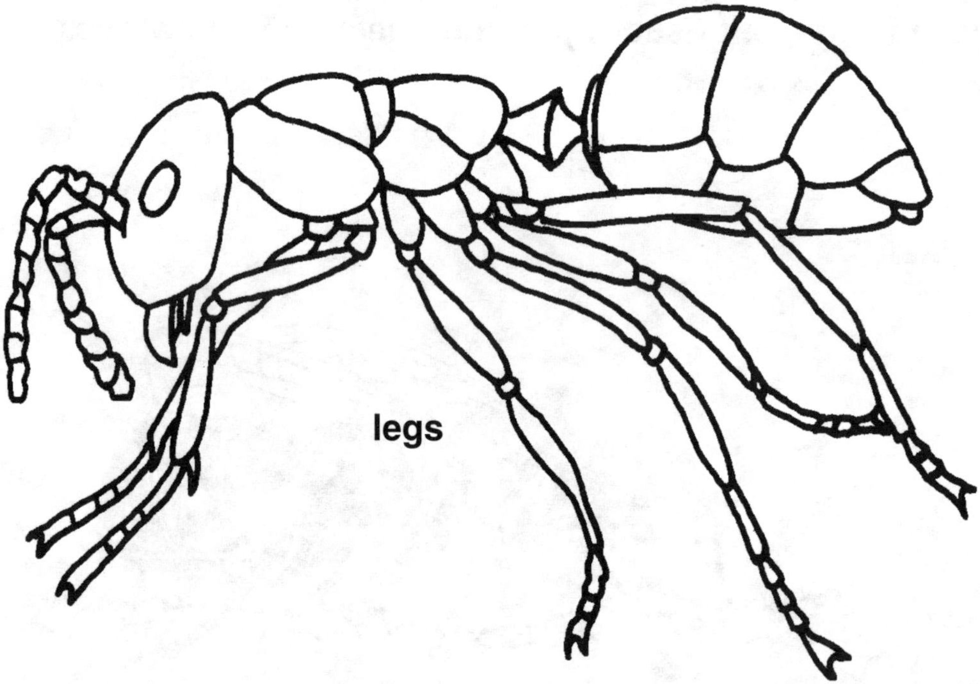

Draw the ants in their tunnels.

Make sure they each have a head, a body (a thorax), an abdomen, and legs. How many legs should you draw?

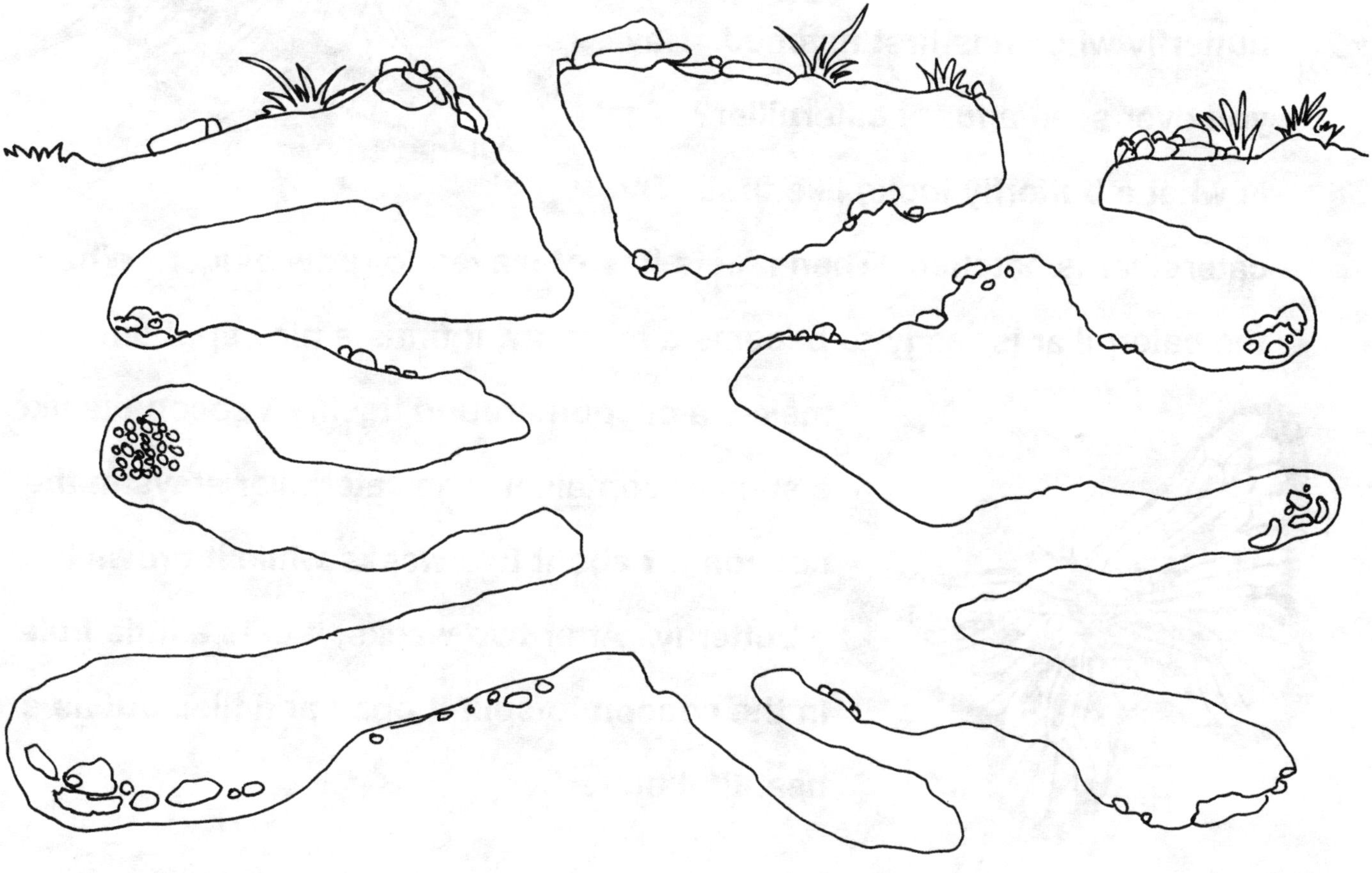

Butterflies

The butterfly is a very interesting insect. It does not look like a beautiful butterfly when it is first hatched. Have you ever seen a fuzzy caterpillar? That is what a butterfly looks like first. The caterpillar is hatched. Then it eats lots of leaves to grow bigger. When the caterpillar is ready to become a butterfly, it finds a nice spot and makes a cocoon around itself. A cocoon is like a shell or container. The caterpillar stays in the cocoon for about two weeks while it grows into a butterfly. After two weeks, it eats a little hole in the cocoon to split it open and flies out as a beautiful butterfly.

Identifying the Stages of the Butterfly

Place a 1 next to what happened first. Place a 2 next to what happened second. And place a 3 next to what happened last.

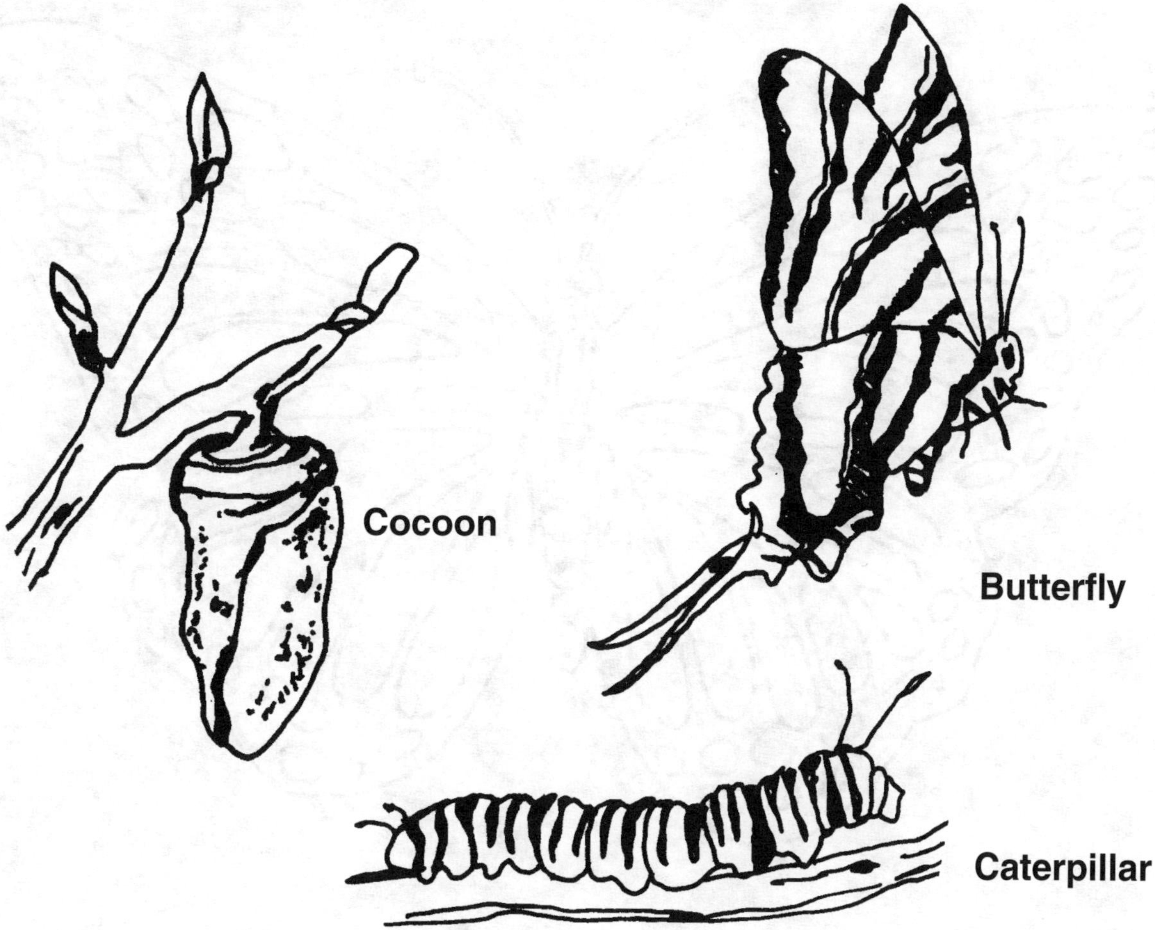

Color the picture of the butterfly. Use lots of colors.

You can Make a Picture of a Butterfly

What you need:

- construction paper (Lighter colors work best.)
- liquid paints (Tempra type)
- scissors
- smock
- black marker or crayon or one black chenille stick (pipe cleaner)

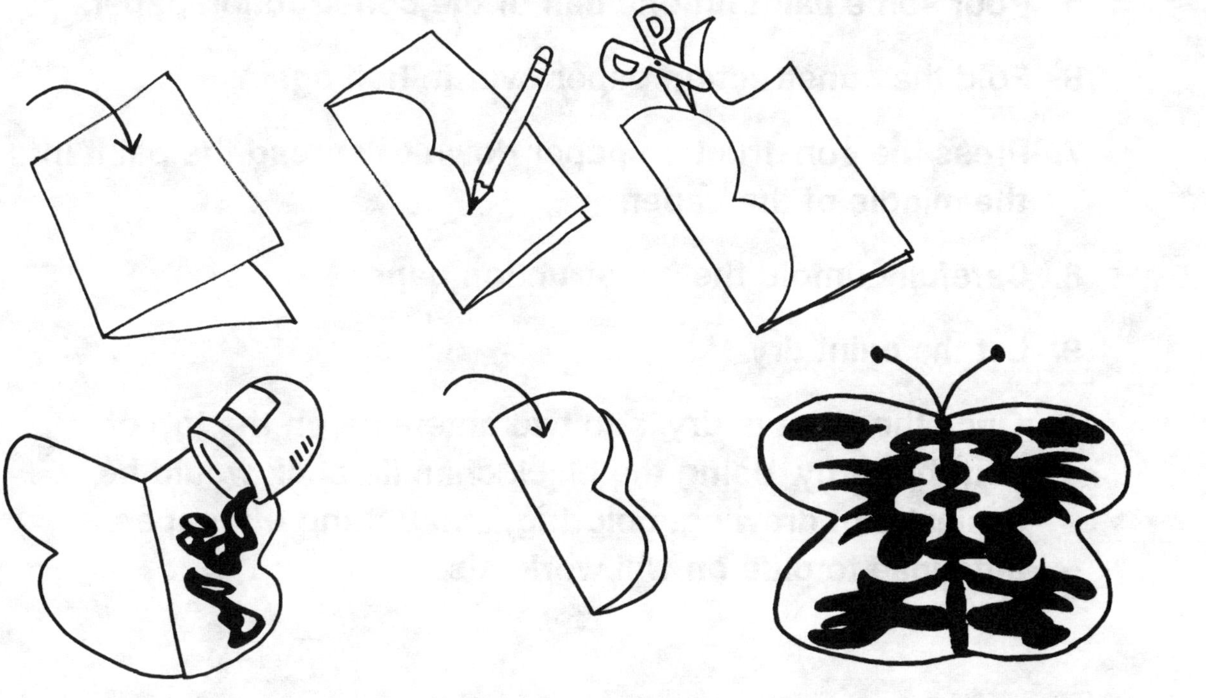

What to do:

1. Put the smock on to protect your clothes from the paint.
2. Fold the construction paper in half.
3. Draw a silhouette of half a butterfly on one side of construction paper.
4. Cut the construction paper. Open the paper. It should look like a butterfly.
5. Pour some paint on one half of the construction paper.
6. Fold the construction paper over in half again.
7. Press the construction paper down to spread the paint in the middle of the paper.
8. Carefully unfold the construction paper.
9. Let the paint dry.
10. Once the paint is dry, add two antennae on the top of your butterfly. Using the black chenille stick would be easiest, but drawing, coloring, and cutting out paper antennae to glue on will work, also.

Identifying the Parts of a Butterfly

Place the correct letter next to the name of the butterfly part.

wing ____________

antennae ____________

body (thorax) ____________

head ____________

abdomen ____________

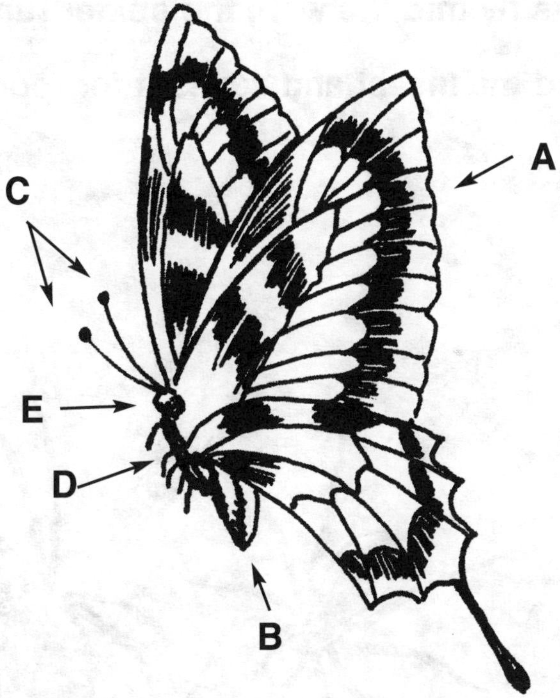

Spiders

Spiders seem a lot like insects, but they are not. Insects have only six legs, but spiders have eight legs. Spiders also have only two body parts: a head and a body. Spiders spin webs to catch their food. When insects fly into the web, the spider runs out onto the web to spin a trap around the insect and saves it for food.

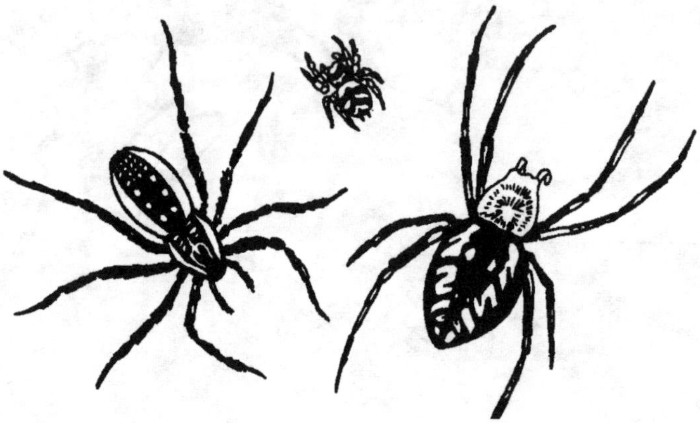

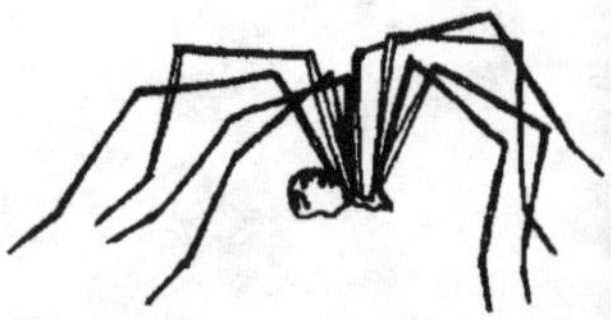

Make a Spider

What you need:

- a small Styrofoam ball
- a larger Styrofoam ball
- a toothpick
- eight black chenille sticks (pipe cleaners)
- three plastic wiggle eyes
- craft glue

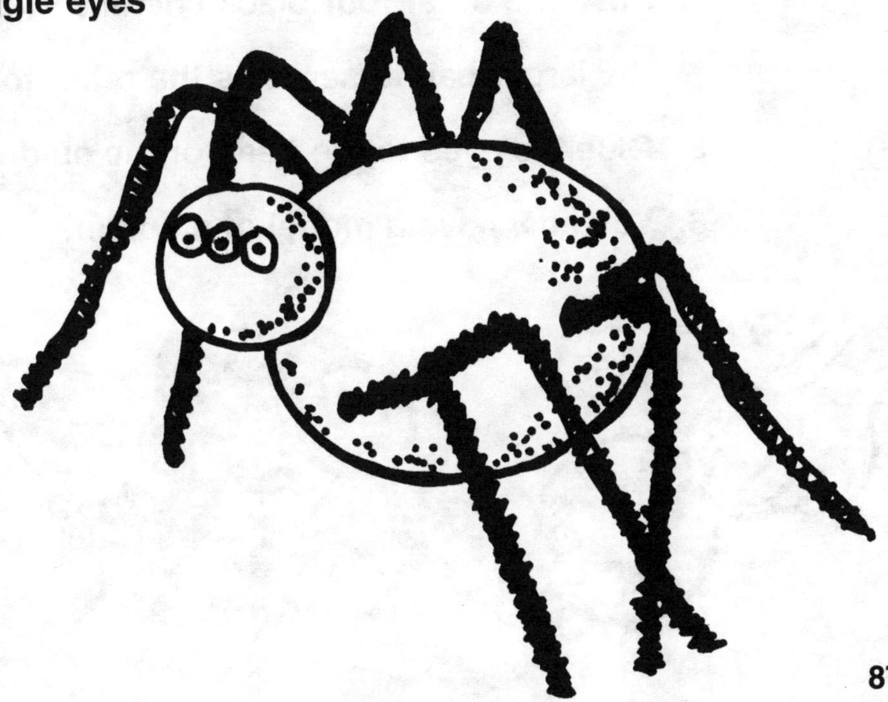

What to do:

1. Push the toothpick into the small Styrofoam ball.
2. Push the larger Styrofoam ball onto the other side of the toothpick until you cannot see the toothpick anymore.
3. Push four of the black chenille sticks (pipe cleaners) into the larger ball on one side to serve as legs for the spider.
4. Push the other four black chenille sticks into the other side of the larger ball to serve as the other four legs.
5. Glue the eyes to the head of the spider.
6. You now have a model of a spider.

Name the Mammal or Insect

Put an X by all the insects and color all the animals. Write the name of the mammal or insect.

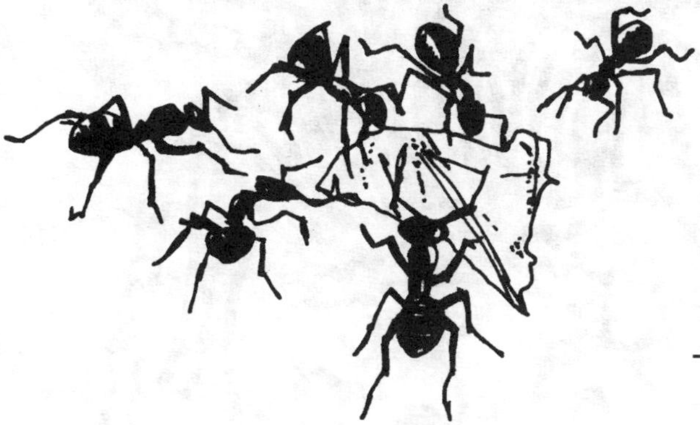

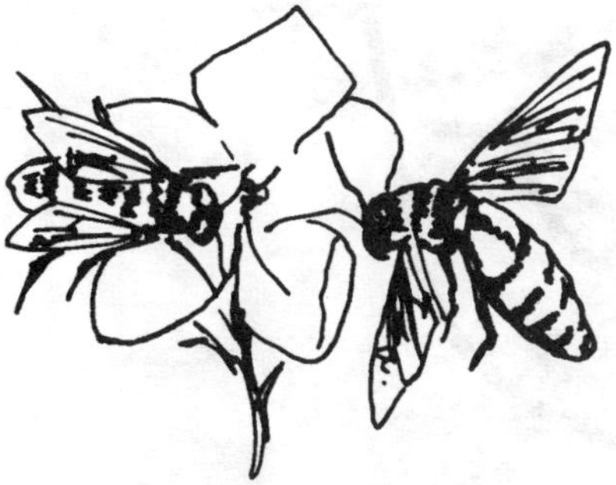

Your Face

Color the face parts on page 91. Cut the face parts out.

Glue or paste them where they belong on the blank faces on page 93. Use yarn for hair.

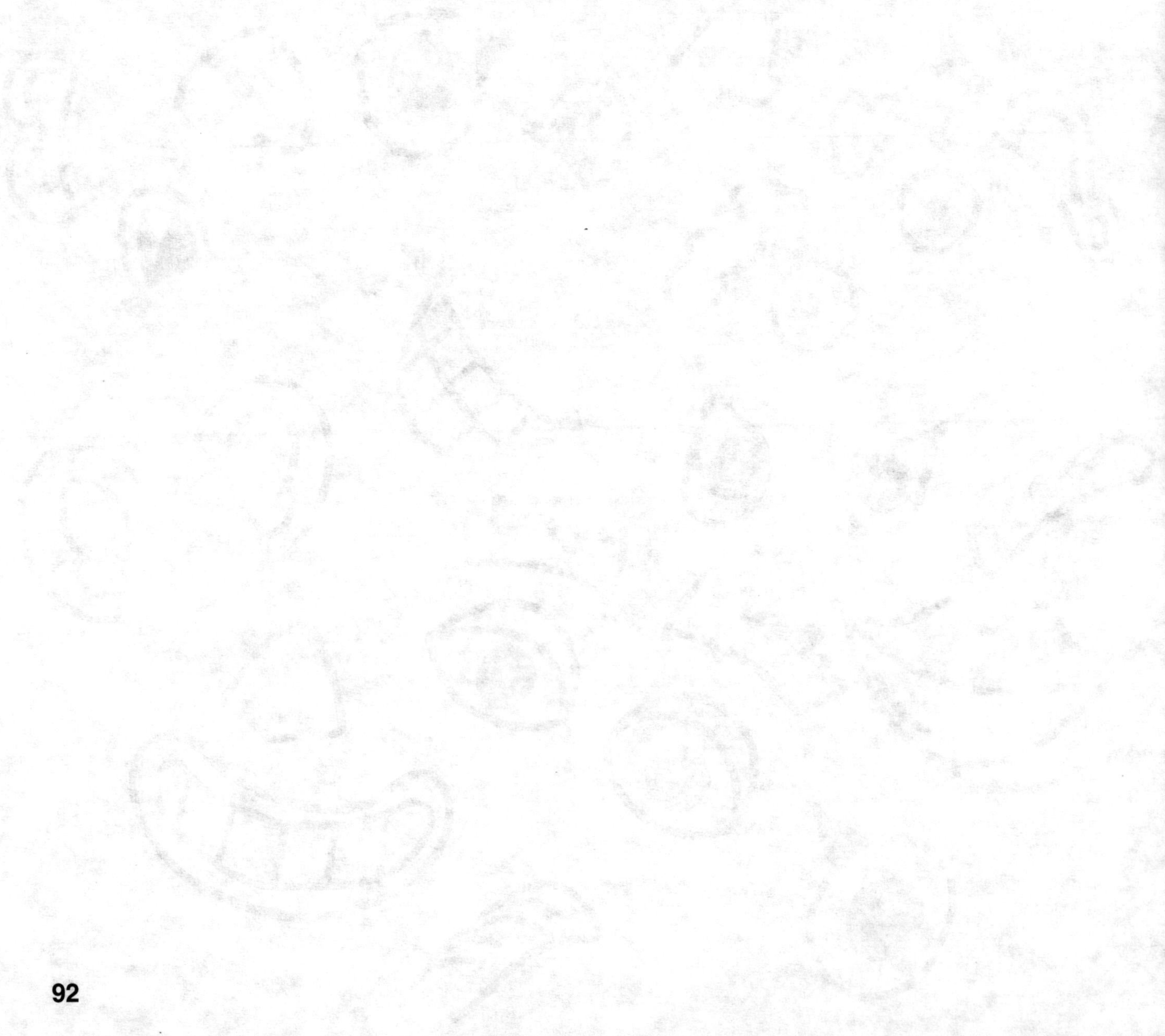

Our Bodies

What you need:

- 9 metal paper fasteners
- crayons or colored pencils
- yarn
- glue or paste
- patterns shown on the following pages
- scissors

What to do:

1. Color the body parts on the next pages.
2. Cut out the body parts.
3. Have an adult help you use the metal fasteners to attach the body parts to each other at the X.
4. Cut yarn for hair.
5. Glue the hair to the top of the head.
6. Use crayons to draw a face on the head.

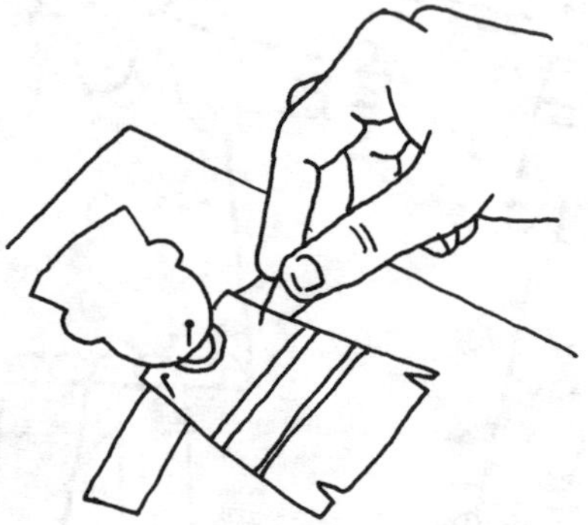

My Picture of Me

What you need:

- butcher paper or several large sheets of newsprint taped together
- crayons or markers
- scissors
- masking tape

What to do:

1. Lay down on the butcher paper.
2. Have someone else draw around your body with a crayon or marker.
3. Carefully get up so you don't tear the paper.
4. Use the crayons or markers to draw in your eyes, ears, mouth, nose, eyebrows, glasses if you wear them, fingers, shoes, and clothes.
5. When you are finished coloring yourself, carefully cut it out on the lines.
6. Have an adult help you hang your image.

Identifying your Body Parts

Draw a line from the word to the correct part of the body in the picture.

head

elbow

chest

thigh

ear

hand

foot

toe

Identifying your Body Parts

Draw a line from the name of the body part to the correct location on the pictures.

chin

back

cheeks

stomach

The Five Senses

Draw a line to the part on your body that you would use for each of these senses.

seeing

hearing

smelling

tasting

touching

Sense of Smell Questions

Circle the things you can do because of your sense of smell.

1. Enjoy the smell of a rose.
2. Tell from another room if dinner is burning.
3. See beautiful colors.
4. Feel a bumpy rock.
5. Enjoy a beautiful sunset.
6. A car tank being filled with gasoline.

Nutrition

In order to grow and be healthy, you need to eat the right foods. Every day you should eat plenty of fruits and vegetables. You should also eat sources of protein, such as meat, eggs, or beans. Breads are good for you, too, and don't forget to drink some milk each day. You should not eat a lot of sweets.

Identifying healthy foods

Circle the meals and snacks that are good for you to eat.

Healthy Snacks

Make Ants on a Log

What you need:

- celery
- peanut butter
- raisins
- butter knife or plastic knife
- an adult helper

What to do:

1. Wash your hands.
2. Rinse a stalk of celery.
3. Have an adult cut the celery into pieces about 3 inches long.
4. Carefully spread peanut butter in the hollow part of each celery log with the knife.
5. Stick raisins (ants) into the peanut butter.
6. Clean up your mess.
7. Eat and enjoy.

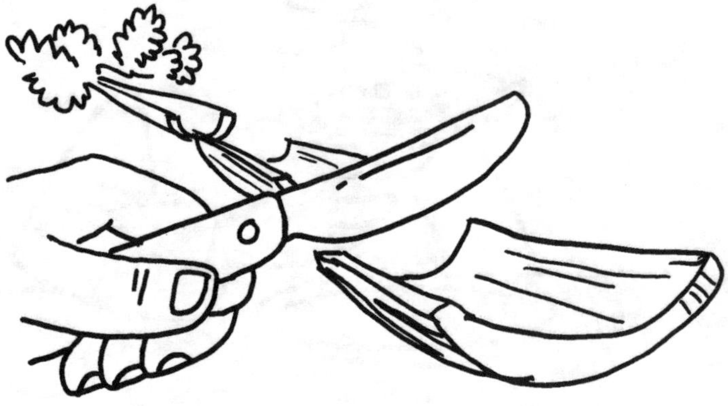

Rest and Exercise

We also need plenty of exercise and rest for our bodies to grow and be healthy. Exercise can be fun to do. Walking, running, hopping, jumping, and most playing outside is exercise.

Rest

But after we exercise our bodies can get very tired and we need some rest. We should all sleep between eight and ten hours each night. Sometimes, if we have been extra busy during the day, we may need a little rest for a short time in the afternoon.

Exercise

What you need:

- stopwatch or wristwatch with a second hand
- empty milk jugs
- chairs
- string

What to do:

1. Make an obstacle course outside. Rinse out the milk jugs, fill them with water. Set up milk jugs to weave between, run around, or hop over. Tie string between two chairs to make an obstacle to go under. Use any other ideas you may have. Be creative.
2. Have an adult time you as you complete the obstacle course.
3. Race against a friend or try to improve your own time.

The more you do it, the better you will get at it and the more exercise you will get.

Safety

If we didn't have safety rules, we would get hurt a lot more often. Nobody likes to get hurt. This is why we should always follow the safety rules. Adults usually tell us how to do things or do some things for us because we haven't grown big enough to know the safest ways to do things. When we grow bigger, we will help those who are younger to stay safe, too.

Identifying Safety

Put an X by the pictures in which the children are not practicing safety.

A boy holding a grandfather's hand as he crosses the street.

A very young girl in the kitchen using a knife to cut an apple.

A slide with two children on it at one time.

Growing Up

What you need:

- two empty coffee cans
- a nail
- a hammer
- strong string or twine
- scissors

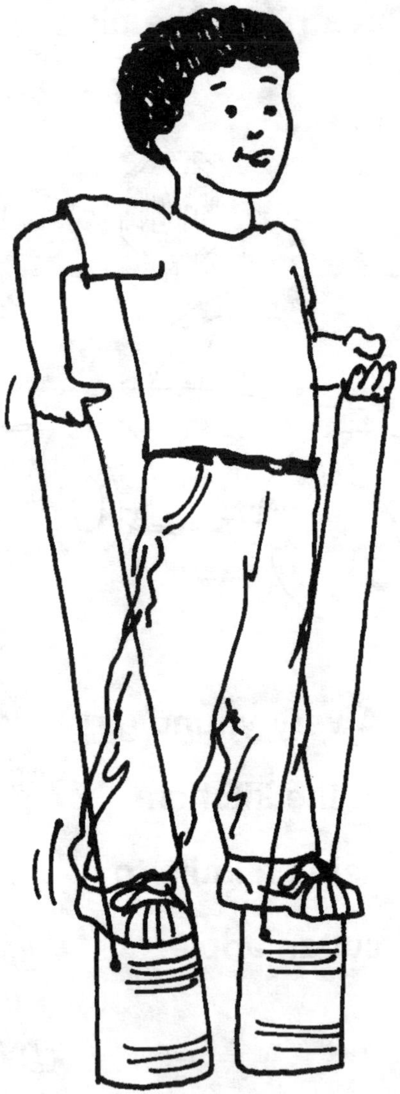

What to do:

1. Have an adult punch a hole in each side of the bottom of each coffee can with the hammer and nail.
2. Measure and cut two pieces of string as long as you are tall.
3. Thread one piece of string through the holes in one coffee can and tie the ends together in a knot.
4. Repeat step three for the other string and coffee can.
5. Stand on the coffee cans while holding onto the string loops. Make sure you are wearing your shoes.
6. Practice walking. You will get better with practice.

Is it fun growing up all at once?

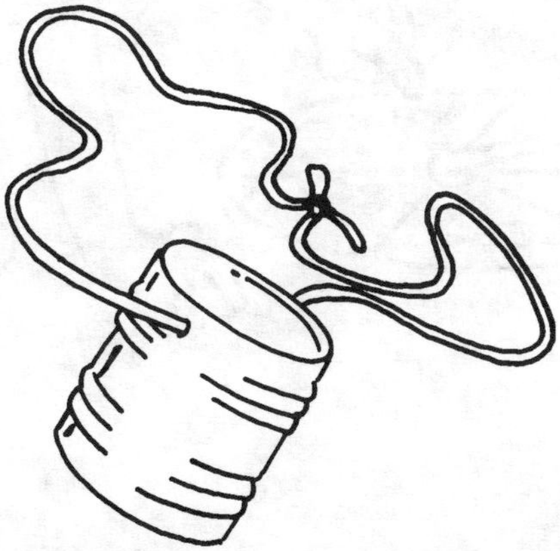

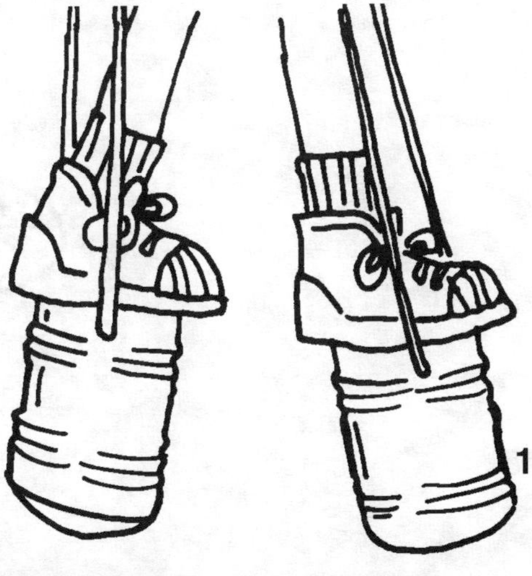

Weather Spin Chart

What you need:

- a metal paper fastener
- next page
- thin cardboard
- paste or glue
- scissors
- crayons or colored pencils

Weather Chart

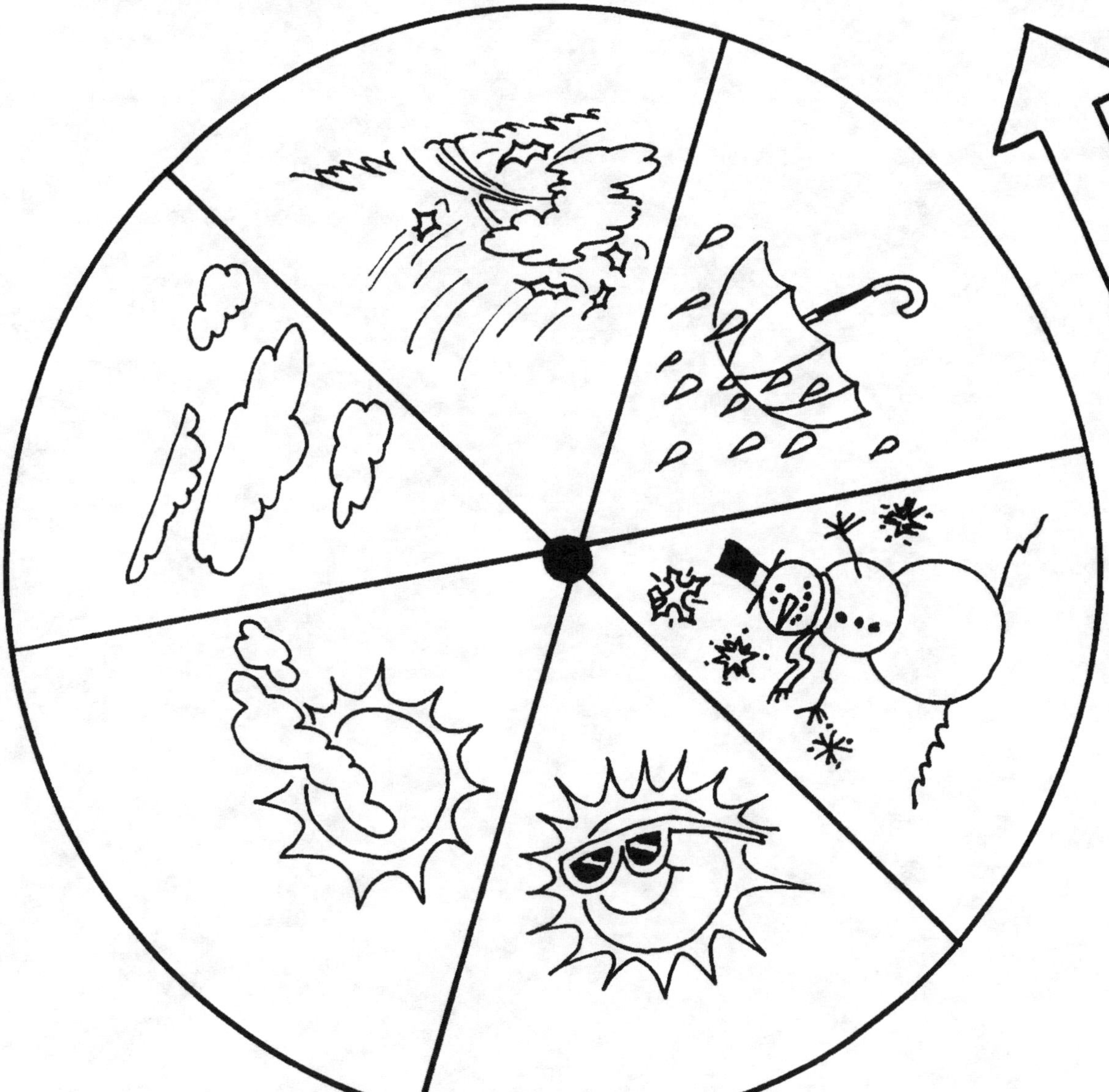

Spinner Pointer

What to do:

1. Color the weather chart and spinner pointer if you wish.
2. Carefully cut out the circle weather chart on the solid line.
3. Carefully cut out the spinner pointer on the solid line.
4. Paste or glue the weather chart to a piece of cardboard.
5. Cut the cardboard around the weather chart.
6. Paste or glue the pointer to a piece of cardboard.
7. Cut the cardboard around the pointer.
8. Carefully push the metal fastener through the dot on the pointer.
9. Continue pushing the metal fastener through the dot on the weather chart.
10. Turn the spinner pointer to the weather you observe outside each day.

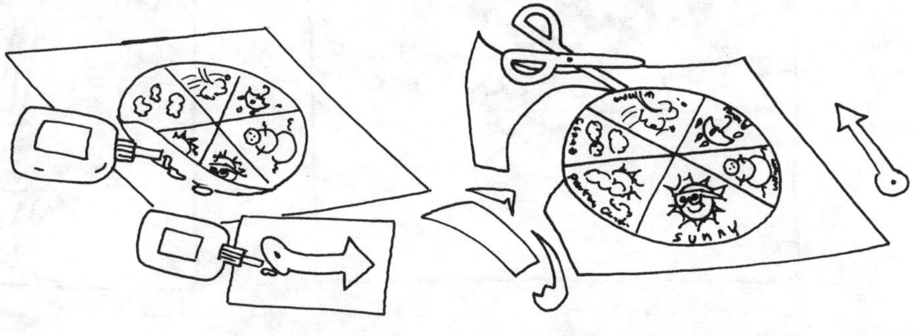

The Seasons

There are four seasons in the year. The first season is winter. Winter is usually colder than summer. Snow falls in winter in some places. Some places do not get cold enough for snow. Still the weather there is usually cooler in winter than at other times during the year.

The next season is spring. Spring is a usually warmer than winter. The wind will blow more often. Spring is often a good time of year to fly kites. There may be more rain in spring than at other times. The spring rain waters the flowers that are blooming.

Next comes summer. The weather can get very hot during the summer. This is a good time of year to go to the beach or to a swimming pool. We play outside a lot during the summer. The summer usually has a lot of bright sunny days.

The last season is special because it has two names. Fall is also called autumn. The leaves in some areas change colors and fall off the trees in the fall. The weather gets a bit cooler.

The Environment

Your environment is the area around you. It could be your room, your school, your house, or your neighborhood. We should always try to take care of our environment. We can make sure our environment is cleaned up of all trash and things are in their proper place. If we take care of our environment, then other people and even animals can enjoy it, too.

Making Your Environment Better

Make a list of some of the ways you can make your environment better.

1. ______________________________

2. ______________________________

3. ______________________________

4. ______________________________

5. ______________________________

Answers

Possible answers. Remember, accept any reasonable response. Children should be encouraged to be creative. If they come up with an interesting new response, check it out together.

Page

10. | | |
|---|---|
| riding bike | boy |
| flying kite | girl |
| eating nut | squirrel |
| in pond | ducks |

11.
1. 2 trees
2. 3 flowers
3. 4 (including 3 ducks)
4. 1 mother duck, 2 ducklings
5. 1 frog

14.
1. 2 pails
2. 2 shovels (The child might infer there is a shovel in the bucket. This is a good place to discuss inferring or making a guess based on information.)
3. 4 children (The child might infer the person in the sailboat is another child.)
4. 1 sand castle

15-17. Colors will vary depending on children.
Shapes can be sorted by triangle, circle, square/rectangle.
Shapes can be sorted by those with dots.
Shapes can be sorted by those with +s.
Shapes can be sorted by those that are plain.
Children may come up with other ways to sort.
Accept any reasonable classification rationale.

19. Soccer balls, baseballs, footballs, basketballs.
Children might also sort by round or not round.
Sometimes they come up with interesting sorting rationale.

21.

Living	Non-Living
grass	a crayon
a plant	a book (came from a tree or trees)
a weed	a spoon (if wooden, could have come from a tree)
	a toy (wooden could have come from a tree)
	a shoe (leather could have come from an animal)
	a pencil (wooden could have come from a tree)

22. A twig was alive at one time. This is a good place to compare to some other things from page 21 that might have been alive at one time. For example, wood comes from trees and pencils are made of wood.

23. Differences: glasses/no glasses, butterfly/bee, 3 flowers/2 flowers, pants/shorts, long sleeves/short sleeves.

24. Differences: no ribbon/ribbon, design on watering can, shoes/barefoot, pant straps/no pant straps, 2 buttons/1 button, water/no water

25. Watch that the children don't pick up poison ivy, poison oak,or poison sumac.

28-29. Answers will depend on the kinds of leaves collected. Accept all reasonable comparisons.

31. Answers are a "toss of the coin."

33. horse-pony, dog-puppy, cow-calf, cat-kitten with ball, bear-cub

34. cat-meow, cow-moo, pig-oink, dog-ruff-ruff

41. birds: parakeet on limb and duck-pg.35, eagle-pg. 37, goldfinch-pg.39

42. fish: trout and salmon-pg.37, bass and perch-pg.39

43. mammals: puppy and pig-pg.35, cow-pg. 37, horse-pg. 39

44. reptiles: iguana-pg.37, crocodile-pg.39
amphibians: frog-pg. 37, salamander-pg. 39
(Accept reptile-children can confuse salamanders for lizards.) Children may have trouble with the difference between reptiles and amphibians. Amphibians have to have water to lay their eggs. Frogs, toads, newts, and salamanders are amphibians. Reptiles lay eggs with leathery shells. They usually have skin covered with scales. Snakes and lizards, turtles and tortoises, crocodiles and alligators, and tuataras are reptiles.

Answers

Page

46. Kangaroo and rabbits hop. They can walk, too.
Snakes slither. Whales swim.
Giraffes walk or run.

47. Leopards and wolves run.
Birds fly and can walk or run.
Frogs jump, leap, and swim.
Dolphins and porpoises swim.

48. Birds and bats fly. Birds walk and run, too.
Kangaroos hop and walk.
Snakes slither.
Kittens run, walk, leap, and climb.

49. Snakes slither.
Hippopotamuses walk and run sometimes. They can even swim.
Birds fly and can walk.

50. Dolphins, whales, and fish swim.
Birds fly and can walk.
Cats run, walk, leap, and climb.

51. Answers will vary. Accept all reasonable responses. Most plants can capture the sunlight's energy to make food, build up leaves, stems, and roots. Without plants, many other living things could not live.

52. Even though there are no flowers on the trees in these pictures, some trees are flowering trees. Point out fruit trees like apple trees and cherry trees. Many trees flower. Conifers such as pine trees do not flower. Really the only living things in these pictures that are not plants are the girl, the birds, and, obviously, the sky.

54. Some animals eat only plants. Some animals eat plants and other animals. Some animals eat only other animals.

55.
1. Yes, plants produce oxygen.
2. Yes, we can eat some plants, but not all plants. Remind children some plants are poison.
3. No, we need plants very much to live.
4. Yes, grass is a kind of plant.

56.

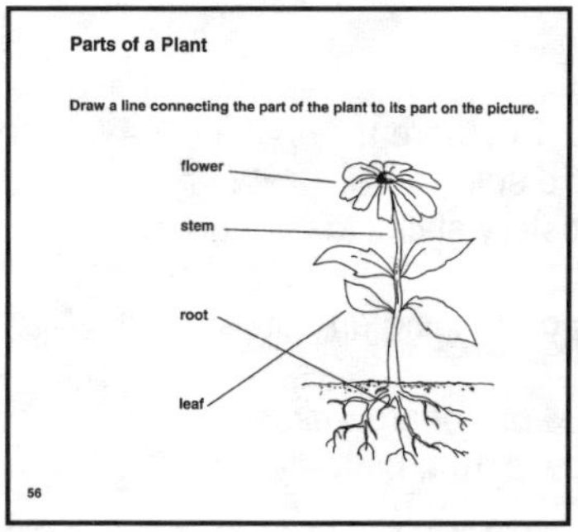

57.

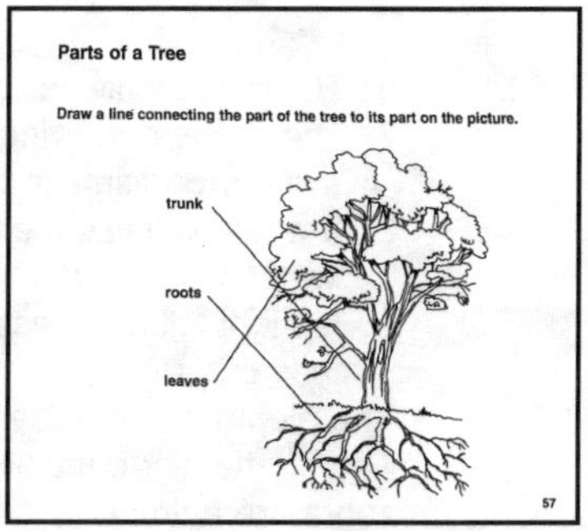

60.
1. They may not see much the first day. The first thing they will see is a root.
2. After a day or two the root should appear.
3. After the root, a small stem should appear with a tiny leaf.
4. The length of time may vary several days.
5. The bean is growing a root and a stem and leaves.
6. Measurements will vary. Stress accuracy in science.

64.
1. The food coloring was absorbed with the water and traveled up the stem of the celery.
2. The celery stalk has tubes that take water through the plant. This is like many vascular plants. The cells in the celery stalk had lost a lot of water. The water moves from plant cell to plant cell until all the cells are filled again.
3. Most plants get water from the soil through their roots.
4. In most plants, the water enters the plant through its roots. (The last part of the celery to get the colored water was the tips of the leaves. The first food-colored water entered the bottom.)

68.
1. This will vary with each child.
2. This will vary depending on the amount of water and sun.
3. The grass the children planted is probably green.
4. No, grass will keep growing. It grows much more slowly when it is cold.
5. No, the eggshell will not grow. It is no longer a part of a living organism.

Answers

Page

69.
6. The grass is living.
7. The soil is non-living. But there may be tiny living organisms in the soil.
8. It would wilt like the celery stalk did. If it got no water, it would die.
9. It might kill the grass depending on how short it was cut.

70. The elephant, snake, and parrot are animals.

71. The giraffe, tiger, monkey, parrot, butterfly, and zebra are animals.

72. Living: tree, flower, fish, and plants in aquarium
Non-living: pencil, book. Remind the children a pencil and a book are made from trees.

73. Living: bear, cat, dog, bird
Non-living: chair and balloon. If the chair is wooden, it came from a tree.

74. Living: horse, grasshopper
Non-living: running shoe, bat, football. Remind the children that if the bat is wood, it probably came from a tree at one time.

75. Living: octopus
Non-living: car, bike, sandwich. But discuss the sandwich. Where did the cheese come from? Where did the bread come from? Is the lettuce still alive? Encourage the children to ask questions.

78.

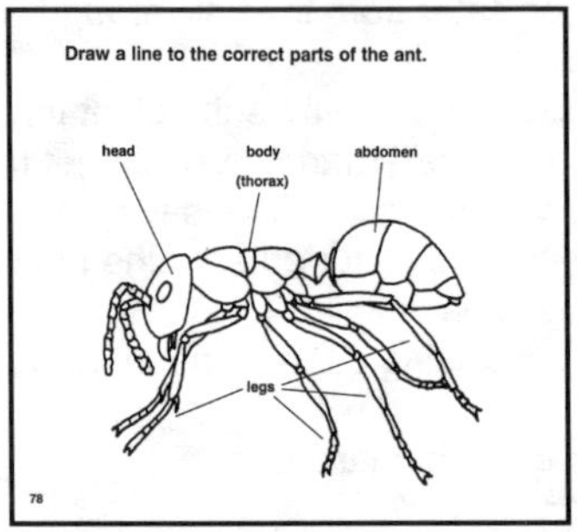

79. The children should draw six legs.

81. caterpillar=1; cocoon=2; butterfly=3

85. A = wing, B = abdomen, C = antennae, D = body, E = head

89. insects: ants, bees, moths
mammals: rats, dogs, cats

103.

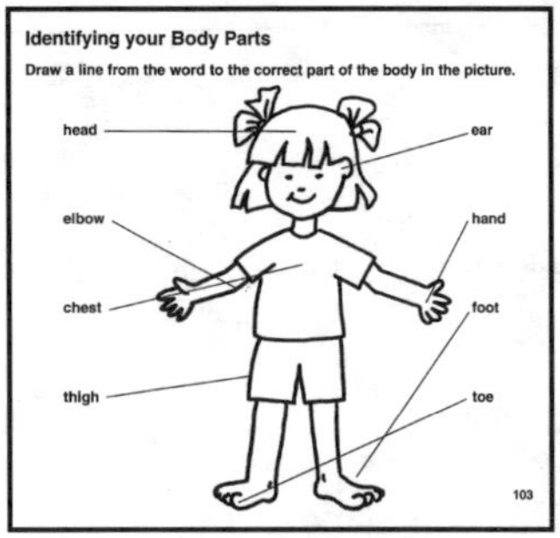

104.

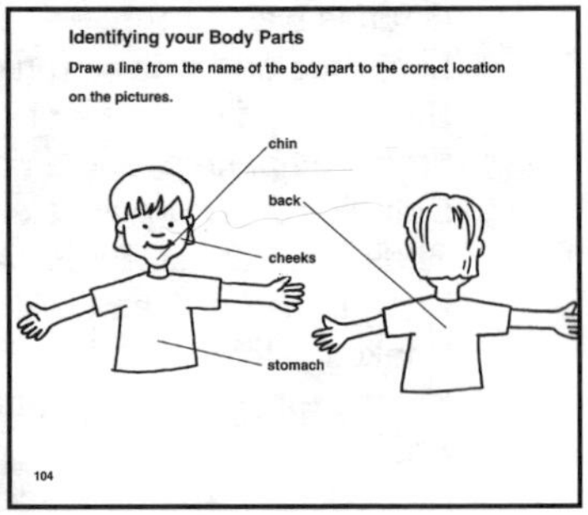

105. seeing - eyes; hearing - ears; smelling - nose; tasting - tongue; touching - hands (But we can feel with other parts of the body, too.)

106. SMELL: 1. smell a rose; 2. tell if dinner is burning (Ask if they could hear if dinner is burning if the cook yells and complains.) 6. smell gasoline
SEE: 3. see colors; enjoy a sunset; 6. see a car being filled with gasoline.
TOUCH: 4. feel a bumpy rock

108. Healthy meals and snacks: breakfast of eggs, bacon, grapefruit, and milk; lunch of sandwich with vegetables and cheese, along with milk or juice; dinner of peas, chicken, mashed potatoes, and a salad; an apple
Questionable snacks include soda or pop, chocolate bar, donut.

115. Safe activities: boy walking with grandfather.
But, obviously, children need to be cautioned to stay away from strangers.
Unsafe activities: two children on a slide at the same time; a girl using a knife to cut an apple.

125. Answers will vary. Here are some possible answers: Recycle and reuse. Pick up trash. Use less water. Use less electricity. Walk more. Use less gasoline. Try not to use too many synthetic products that are not recycled. Car pool with friends.